From the Vetch F Libert:

Biography

This book is the second poem book I've had published, the last one was called "I can only be me" which Angel Rangel bought, well his wife Nicola did.
This book was started as a Swansea City poem book, then I wrote a poem about Cardiff City that wound them right up, so I did a few more, it's a poem book based on my love and passion for Swansea City, where I'm a Season ticket holder, there are a few Cardiff ones in there. There's quite a bit of banter, and I do enjoy winding them up.

I have a poem page www.swanseajackpoet.wordpress.com and my poems are seen and read all around the world from Iraq to Bangladesh from Taiwan to Uganda from Chile to the Philippines, I am spreading the Swansea City word. I've recently been asked if one of my poems from my last book could be performed as part of someones education in Texas. Who would have thought a Jack, who was brought up in the Clase area of Swansea would be helping to educate America.

If your a Swans fan or you know a Swans fan it's an ideal gift, and if you know a Cardiff fan and you want to wind them up, this could be the book you are looking for.

You can follow me on Twitter @tannertimebomb or @SwanseaJackPoet

The things written in the book, are copyright and are protected by copyright law, they are my thoughts, and my sense of humour, it will not be everyone's cup of tea, it will jog your memory and hopefully make you laugh, and feel proud to be a Jack.

Dedication

I started writing poems when my mum died in 1996 when i was 19, that was in 1996. I dedicate this book to my Mother's memory, I doubt very much, she would have thought her baby boy, would have two books published, I have her to thank for my upbringing, and to take part and enjoy sport, and be proud of where I come from. Also my two children, who inspire me every day, my daughter Sophie 18, my son Jackson 18 months, and my partner Nadine, who has proof read the book, so any grammar errors are totally down to her, ha.

My best pal, Gareth Stilwell, who queued for 27 hours for our season ticket, and got us seats where we can hardly see whats going on when the ball is up by the family stand.
Have to give a special mention to my cousin Leigh Griffiths, who designed the cover for both my books, @JustGrif.
The picture on the back cover was drawn by Simon Meyrick, follow @SimonMeyrick, his drawings of the players are outstanding and if you want a picture drawn, he is your man.

To the players and staff at Swansea City F.C.

I would also like to thank my sister Alison, for taking me to my first Swans game in 1980, when I was 4.

And finally to everyone that has bought the book, my feet are on the ground, I'm hardly Dylan Thomas, I was brought up in Clase, and went to Penlan School, I thank you for spending your hard earned cash, or for the people in Cardiff, I appreciate you spending your benefit money. I am hoping to make enough money to buy next years season ticket. I hope you enjoy the book, as I share my recent memories of following the Swans, and I hope you enjoy the good and the bad.

Contents

1. Founded in 1912
2. League Cup Winners
3. Cardiff in the Premier League
4. Chico Flores
5. Fixtures are out
6. Swansea's Spanish Armada
7. Lee Trundle YJB
8. Ferrie Bodde
9. My Little Bony
10. Garry Monk
11. Tom Ince : Why I turned down Cardiff
12. Angel Rangel
13. Vincent Tan & Sam Hamman - Brockback Mountain
14. Swansea 3 Panathanikos 3 - Ode to Dai Dauria
15. Europa League v Malmo
16. Friendly Banter
17. Playing with Lee Trundle
18. www.scfc.co.uk
19. Swans 4 FC Malmo 0
20. Not going to Sweden
21. Swans v Man U preview
22. Transfer Deadline day
23. Cardiff sign Odenwingie
24. Jonjo's Night
25. Leon
26. Cardiff start to the Premier League

27.   Swans Dreaming
28.   In the Cardiff Slums
29.   Valencia v Swans
30.   Swansea win & Cardiff loose
31.   West Ham 3 Cardiff 2 League Cup
32.   Birmingham 3 Swansea 1
33.   Swans v Arsenal
34.   Credit to Cardiff
35.   Supporters Behave
36.   Match Day Vorm
37.   Michu
38.   The painters in
39.   Ashley Williams
40.   Building up to the derby
41.   Derby Day
42.   More Derby Day
43.   So now you want a poem
44.   The Fall Out
45.   Ramsay: Scores and you applaud him
46.   10 Years and its Hull again
47.   Two Nil to the Mighty Palace
48.   Ten Years on
49.   Pink Ferrari Crossbar Challenge
50.   Swansea Dream Team #DreamteamJack

Founded in 1912

Founded in 1912 as Swansea Town
I was there against Hull, when we nearly went down
A hatrick from James Thomas to win 4-2
Back in the day, when Cardiff wore blue
We left behind the Vetch field, our famous ground
The Swans had been bought, for just one pound
Huw Jenkins led us to the Liberty
The new home for Swansea City
We changed our style and passed the ball
It didn't matter Leon Britton was 5 foot tall.
Brendan took us to the play off final where we won 4-2
I drank so much beer, and I bet you did too,
A Scotty Sinclair hatrick took us to the holiest of grails
It's obvious to me, there's only one team in Wales
The first and only Welsh team to grace the premier league
Then in came one of the greatest players of all time
We went from pass masters, to simply....sublime
The man to thank , is Michael Laudrup
Leading us to the final of the Capitol One Cup
When on the 24TH of February
We'll follow our team to Wembley.
Pre match we'll have Kevin Johns
Your only here to watch the Swans,
Hymns & Arias will be sung so loud
The team, will make the Jack Army proud.

The ref will toss a coin, heads or tails?
We've got Ashley Williams...he's captain of Wales.
The swans, the swans will tear you apart again.
We've got players, that have played for Spain,
Pablo Hernandez,
Chico , Chico, Chico Chico Flores
And Angel Rangel, he feeds the homeless.
Singing along to the beat of that drum,
Are you watching Cardiff scum.
Bradford will come at us, we ll need to grit our teeth
We've got Ben Davies, a local lad from Neath,
Standing on the North Bank, way down by the sea
We are internationally famous, thanks to Ki .

We'll sing, drink beer and have lots of fun
Singing the names of Routledge and Jonathon De Guzman.
On the right, we've got Nathan Dyer
The Swans are on form, and the team is on fire
I am predicting another 4-2
A hatrick from our hero, we love Michu
We'll bring the trophy home and have an open top bus parade
Joey Allen & Scott Sinclair wishing they had stayed
Swansea til I die.... The way they are playing makes me happy to be alive
Looking forward to the Europa League, Thursday night, Channel 5
So Take my hand, take my whole life too,
For I can't help, falling in love with you.

League Cup Winners Swansea City

We'll remember that date, the 24th of February
When 33000 jacks travelled to Wembley
We went up by bus, train or by car
We showed Bradford City, who we are
To play under the famous Wembley Arch
The Jack Army went on the march
What more has Leon Britton got to do for an international call up
He's played in every division, and now he's won the League Cup
Leon is a huge player, but the size of a gnome
And Wembley has become, "our second home "
We had Gerhard Tremmel in goal
Wayne Routledge was magic in the hole
"Take me to the Vetch Field, way down by the sea"
We've got Ben Davies and he wears number thirty three
We are Internationally famous, thanks to our Ki.
He was Replacing the injured Chico Flores
And Angel Rangel, he feeds the homeless
Dyer opened the scoring
Which started the jack army roaring
A magic finish from Michu
Took off the pressure, with number two
Pablo Hernandez with an eye of a needle pass
To our Spanish contingent , mucho gracias
A Dyer one two with Routledge at the start of the second half
"We're premier league and were having a laugh"
De Guzman, brought down in the box and they were down to ten
I'd have let Nathan Dyer make history, and take that pen
Jonathon De Guzman, made it four as he put the penalty away
This was going to become the most famous of Swansea City's day
All the fans joined to remember the victims of the Bradford fire
Roland Lamah replaced Nathan Dyer
On came Tiendelli, his first name is Dwight
We'll "build it up, in Black and White"
The Swans performed like they were Brazil
Then De Guzman scored in added time, to make it 5 nil
The Bradford fans sung until the very end
Good luck for the rest of the season, our Northern friend

Ashley Williams led the team up the steps.....all 107
With Besian Idrizaj watching down proud, from heaven
Our Club Captain Gary Monk
"Lets all have a disco," and get drunk
They lifted the trophy together
We'll remember this day forever and ever

It's something you can tell your grand children
Kev Johns prayers had been answered..... Amen
Vorm ,Bartley, Shechter, Kemy , and Luke Moore
We've got Chico Flores, our Spanish Matador
To lift our first major trophy in our Centenary year
I couldn't have been the only one who had a little tear
Maybe a new song by Max Boyce
Swanseas my town by birth, but my club by choice
We sang " Hymns and Arias"
And took the cup home, to the "land of our fathers"
I didn't even read my program
I took it home to show my 9 month old son
When my son grows up
I'll tell him I was there , when we won the League Cup.
He can pass it on from generation to generation
When Swansea City carried the hearts of a nation
"From the Vetch Field to the Liberty", we'll keep the Jack flag flying high
"I'll be Standing on the North Bank, til the day I die."

I hope they give Laudrup, the keys to the city
And Huw Jenkins hands him a Europa kitty?
We wonder now who Michael Laudrup can lure
"As we are all going on a European tour"
They lined the streets in their thousands from Kingsway to the Guildhall
This squad will go down in history, as the greatest of them all.
An open top bus & A victory parade
Who will we draw ? Red Star Belgrade?
We'll be excited for the draw, and we'll always carry hope
Swansea City, could go "to Rome to see the pope"
The Europa League will be tough
And "I just can't get enough"
I'm excited for next season already, I'm not going to lie
I am Swansea, " Swansea til I die "
We'll travel across Europe, by plane, bus or rail
We've got players from Germany, Holland and even Israel,
South Korea, England, Wales & Spain
Wanting to play for our Greatest Dane.
"So Take my hand, take my whole life too,
For I can't help, falling in love with you. "
A new chapter in our history, waiting to be written
I'm in love with Swansea City and I'm totally smitten.

Cardiff in the Premier League

Finally you made it to the holy grail
Cardiff City they usually fail
It's time for you to enjoy your day
After Swansea City showed you the way
Yet another boring nil, nil
Next year you'll be outclassed by our silky skill
So welcome to the Premier League to our Welsh " Chums"
Hope there's enough dead rats to go round the Cardiff slums
You finally get to play with the big boys
Maybe in your stadium you'll finally make some noise

A Welsh derby to look forward to
Remember when you played in blue
You had morals then but you sold your soul
I wouldn't use your shirt, as bog roll
We'll turn you over in Legoland
When you come to us don't forget your arm band
We get to watch you swim away
And laugh at the way that you play
Be careful in the River Tawe not to drown
When next year we send you back down
We get to watch the Cardiff ship sink
Next year you'll probably end up playing in pink
Every week for you a big occasion
Remember you're not Welsh, but Malaysian

I remember when we made a fuss
You don't belong in the same league as us
We are Swansea, Swansea til I die
It won't be long, til they sack Malky Mackay
You can only dream of being us
I bet your relegated by Christmas
You sing " You Jack bastards, we're coming for you "
You'll soon be bankrupt, and propping up League Two

Chico Flores

We've taken to him like he's one of our own
Devastated when he broke a bone
He missed playing in the Cup Final at Wembley
The number 4 for Swansea
We sing his name Chico
Four men went to mow
Went to mow a meadow
3 men 2 men 1 man and his dog Jack
He's our famous centre back
Step over lollipops in attack
Chico Chico Chico Flores he wears his heart on his sleeve
When he plays , we all believe
Our very own Spanish Matador
Someone we've grown to adore
Watch Chico you'll never be bored
The winner of last seasons newcomer award
In many a game he has starred
We love you Chico, you Jack Bastard.

The Fixtures are out 2013/14

The fixtures are out and I can't wait
August 17th that special date
Like you I am excited
To the Liberty where we play United
We'll sing and clap and make some noise
Man U led out, by David Moyes
Pitting his wits against Michael Laudrup
We are the holders of the League Cup
So we have nothing to fear
We're established in the top tier
A game sure to be on Sky TV
Cheered on by you and me
We'll sing Hymns and Arias
And welcome new boy Jose Canas
Hopefully there's more signings on the way
But they have to fit in to the structure we pay
The players will still earn a good crust
But in Huw Jenkins, we hold our trust
Tutumlu is full of shit
We're about to unveil our new kit
Captain Ash could say goodbye
But we're all Swansea, Swansea til we die
The season is about to begin
Lets kick it off, with a famous home win

Swansea's Spanish Armada / Armada Española de Swansea

Tenemos siete jugadores de nuestro equipo , translates to mean
We have seven Spanish players in our team
Michael Laudrup has picked out the cream
A football nation, world ranked number one
Who will now play along to the beat of the Liberty drum
They are used to seeing a Spanish bull
They'll experience the Liberty, rocking when full
To break down Swansea City, teams will have to try harder
To get through our ....Spanish Armada
They play for Swansea City
Seven translates to siete
With a strong contingent I'm sure they can gel
Started by our long serving resident Angel Rangel
He feeds the homeless, and he's a local hero
Someone we've all grown to love is Chico
For them the sunshine will vanish
But we could all do with learning, a little Spanish
Tenemos siete jugadores de nuestro equipo
They've come for the style of football, and not for the dough
Eye of a needle passes from Hernandez, Pablo
Laudrup has been backed to spend, by the clubs Top Brass
Great signing, great hair Jose Canas
He could give some of his hair to Jonjo
A young promising midfielder Alejandro Pozuelo
Cant wait for The East Stand's version of Lady Gaga's Alejandro
The saying is its like watching Brazil, it should be like watching Spain
Can they bring some sun, and get rid of this rain
Sombrero is a Spanish Hat
Welcome You Jack Bastard Jordi Amat
And finally last seasons player of the year
Lift your hand bend your fingers and wave to your ear
I love him, and so do you
We will, we will, Michu
We are strong in defence and attack
You are now Bastardos de Jack

Lee Trundle you Jack Bastard

The icon is back where he belongs
You remember the man and one of his songs
"Lee Trundle , My Lord"
Back in the day he was all we could afford
We were broke, and we signed him on a free
The guy is a God, to the likes of you and me
He scored on his debut against Bury, down the Vetch
If he played for us now, a fee of £10 million he'd fetch
He scored a hatrick in three league games in a row
His wonder goal against Yeovil, still makes me think WOW
If we struggled in a game he'd show us all a trick
If I had one word to describe Lee Trundle, it would have to be "magic"
He often featured on Soccer AM
Thank God, for our Lee, Amen
The goals you scored for us, thanks for all 83
You'll be remembered as a legend, so thank you Lee.
When we were in the lower leagues you brought the club some fame
"Lee, Lee, Lee Trundle" we'd always sing your name
With Andy Robinson, we all remember that dance
To come back to the club he loves, he jumped at the chance
Give Trundle the ball, and he's sure to score
Good luck in your role, as the Club Ambassador
With my poems, I doubt I'll ever be classed as a Bard
But Welcome home Lee Trundle, You Jack Bastard

Ferrie Bodde

He's had to retire due to injury
Cruciate ligaments gone in his knee
He was our star player in his day
He helped the team to play the Swansea Way
We could have cashed in on his price tag
His own following , he brought from Den Haag
The Den Haag fans were crazy
Following their star Ferrie Bodde
A business decision made to let him go
With all Swansea fans thinking oh no
We remember him dominating in midfield
Each comeback we hoped his knee had fully healed
Sadly it wasn't to be
I hope to see you back at The Liberty
Good luck my Dutch friend
No one here, wanted your career to end
Feel sad for him, but what to say
Thank you for the memories, and good luck Ferrie

My Little Bony

We welcome to the City of Swansea
A striker called Wilfried Bony
The transfer saga ran and ran
But we've finally managed to get our man
With other clubs in the queue
He pulled it off, our main man Huw
Thank God a fee was agreed
Cos It dominated my twitter feed
What the hell was the delay
We'd be checking throughout the day
We all had doubts, will he sign?
Will he buy a house in BONYmaen !
Has he signed yet ? We'd all check on our phones
#DontGoGentleSwans

Signing a top striker was a must
The club delivered, in Huw We Trust
In the Dutch league last year he scored the most
Born in Bingerville on the Ivory Coast
For his National team he's got 8 goals in twenty
For the Swans he's sure , to get plenty
For £14 million a new club record
Down the Liberty where he'll be adored
Last season he averaged a goal every game
And for Swansea City, we'll have more of the same
To the tune of Chesney Hawkes "He is the one and only
Superstar striker Wilfried Bony
He plays for Swansea City
We paid a record fee,
No place he'd rather be,"
Billy Idol's Mony Mony
We've got our man Wilfried Bony
"Here he comes now say Bony Bony
Shoot them down now, Sing Bony Bony "
He's 6 foot tall and he looks real hard
Welcome to Swansea, you Jack Bastard

Garry Monk

When his transfer in 2004 was sealed
We welcomed this man to the Vetch Field
From that season we began our climb
And this is a tribute in the form of a rhyme
He's a legend, that all the fans would like to thank
Down the Liberty & from the terraced North Bank
Thank you for your role in our rise
A hero to us, that's no surprise
Someone to marshal our back four
A Jack forever, an oath that he swore
He'd defend the goals at all cost
The penalty area, the place he bossed
In his first season with Sammy Ricketts, he would bunk
He is our leader, "there's only one Garry Monk"
We all know Sammy Ricketts, is partial for a spew
Garry was there from the start, when his chunks first blew.
He would go onto captain our club in all four divisions
That was one of Kenny Jackett's best decisions
He helped lead us to promotion out of League Two
He helped the Swansea City dream, that keeps coming true
Football League Trophy winners, 2-1 v Carlisle
A trophy in Cardiff, enough reason to smile
The last Welsh team to lift a trophy in Cardiff, enough reason for us to brag
A famous day, with Alan Tate and his flag
That night I met one of our centre backs
Celebrated with them in Jumpin Jaks
Then onto a different style of football under Roberto Martinez
League One Champions , a record points haul, answered all of our prayers
Thank you Garry for everything you do
We won the Championship play off final, four goals to two
We were 3-0 up, and the foot came off the throttle
Went to 3-2 and they were testing our bottle
They hit the post, my nails were being bitten
The ball fell to Hunt, and I thought I'd had a kitten
It was a certain goal, I glanced up at the clock
Then in slid Captain Fantastic with a right foot block
He led us up the stairs, there was no prouder Swan
All the players wearing shirts with Besian Idrizaj on
I had a tear in my eye,
We're in the Premier League...I'm "Swansea til I die "
Able to read the game, like he has a sixth sense
The heart and the rock of our defence.

A natural leader of men,
Someone to round the troops when " We only had ten men"
"Na na na na nana na Garry Gary Monk
Garry Monk, Garry Garry Monk"
He has decided to hand over the club captains armband
So, " Take my hand,"
"Take my whole life too,
For I can't help, falling in love with you"
A true professional, and he always does the right thing
A starring role for Garry from a Jack to a King
Loved by the crowd down the Liberty
When he leaves they should retire his jersey
We aren't at that stage just yet,
At least one more season, I would like to bet
I've followed his career, with intrigue
He captained us in the Premier League
He's played under Jackett & Kevin Nugent
And when our transformation underwent
Martinez, Sousa, Brendan & Laudrup
A winner of the Capitol One Cup
He led us up the steps at Wembley
A proud club captain, of Swansea City
A League Cup win five nil, at a canter
He joined Twitter, Monk loves the banter
Someone to depend upon, that is for sure
And about to embark on a European Tour
Swansea the place we all live,
His autobiography says it all, 'Loud, Proud & Positive'
In Swansea's history the best captain there's ever been
Thank You Garry Monk , Swansea's Number Sixteen

Tom Ince on why I turned down Cardiff

An £8million fee agreed for the Blackpool wing
And after three weeks of almost begging
I just read a quote from Tom Ince
The thought of playing for Cardiff made me wince
My dad is taking out a restraining order
I'd rather stay in the championship, than transfer.
Everyone knows Cardiff will go down
That guy Vincent Tan, what an absolute clown
As you can see from the smile on my face
It's cos I won't have to go back to that God forsaken place
I'd rather stay at Blackpool with my Dad and my chums
Than move to the Cardiff slums
The thought of playing for Malky Mackay
I've got to admit it, I'm Swansea til I die

Angel Rangel

He helped kick start the Swans going up
He has won the Capitol One Cup
When we struggled there were offers to take him away
Bigger clubs, offering bigger pay
To Swansea City, he's always stayed true
Angel Rangel our number 22
Watch he plays the second half of a game in long sleeve
When he joined I don't think he'd realise what he'd achieve
A premier league defender in his own right
He helped build us up in black and white
An excellent defender , playing at right back
Solid defender, who loves to attack
Bombing forward, comfortable on the ball
Swansea's greatest right back ? That would be my call
He gave up the weather in sunny Spain
A proud moment when he led us out, A leader, A Captain
He met a local girl, and made her his wife
Had children and settled here for the rest of his life
A local hero feeding the homeless people of Swansea
On and off the field, a hero and role model for you and me
Now there are 8 Spaniards in our team,
Now he's embarking on a European dream
He's a Jack, he's helping them feel at home, so they can gel,
There's only one.... Angel Rangel

Vincent Tan and Sam on Brockback Mountain

The people of Cardiff say I'm obsessed
Up in the capital, it's become a sausage fest
What more about Cardiff is there to say,
If Vincent Tan was my leader , then I'd swim away.
Cardiff have finally got someone to sign
Unfortunately it's Sam Hamman this time
They've finally made up from their lovers tiff
Known as the Bromance of Cardiff
First he made you all turn red
Now he's got Sam, back in his bed.
Vincent Tan is taking the piss
Sam & Tan reminisce about their first kiss
It was under the floodlights at Ninian Park
Only the rats there watching from the dark
To frightened to speak up from the sewer
Barbecued dead rat, served on a skewer
Cardiff City are in a right state
Even the rats, can't take much more of his bait
For the last few years he's made Cardiff fans look like fools
They don't deserve that, even though they're all tools
Turned down by Wanayama and Tom Ince
The thought of Sam & Tan, makes my stomach wince
They take turns going down on each other
It's normal in Cardiff, when your fathers your brother
We can't stop laughing at you down the road
A laughing stock, but we'll never get bored
So Vincent Tan has got a rent boy
A 12 inch vibrator their favourite sex toy
Anal beads they are just for fun
Sam "Wash your mouth out son,"
Soon you'll get your turn
Cardiff City, will you ever learn
Vincent Tan is out of his depth, he's lost the plot
With Sam Hamman they've tied the knot
Still trying to sign someone, they've tried and tried
Sam Hamman doesn't count, he's just Vincent's Thai bride

Swansea 3 Panathanikos 3
Ode to Dai D'Auria

Last time we played in Europe was down the Vetch
In the last minute the ball went passed Lee Bracey's outstretch
Panithanikos broke our heart
After Robbie James & Andy Melville had torn them apart
We had Chris Coleman Tommy Hutchinson & John Salako
We were out of the Cup after a 3-3 draw
It was 1989, I was there,
Dai D'auria in those days had a little hair
A trivia question for a quiz in a pub
Who was the last player to come on for the Swans as a European sub ?
That was our last European game
Swansea born Dai D'auria remember the name?

Europa League v Malmo

Now we are back to take Europe by storm
Will Laudrup start Tremmel or will he play Vorm ?
Our season is about to begin
Be great to start it off with a European win
A Europa League qualifier,
We've got Pablo, Routledge & Dyer
New additions added Canas & Bony
We welcome them all to the City of Swansea
Angel Rangel at full back,
Will he start with Michu & Bony in attack
A Liberty debut for Jonjo ?
Will he start Jordi Amat or Pozuelo
Add them to favourites like Leon & Chico
As we take on FC Malmo
They are a team from Sweden
Will he start with Neil Taylor, or go with Ben ?
Will it be Ash or Garry Monk to lead as out
The squad has improved, of that there's no doubt
We'll welcome them to play the best team in Wales
When I think of Sweden I think Blondes in pigtails....
Beautiful blondes like Ulrika Jonsson
Sven, Sven, Sven Goran Eriksson
Anders Frisk the football ref
To Hurty Gurty the Muppet Chef
He'd make Miss Piggy meatballs for dinner
Bjorn Borg a five time Wimbledon winner
Abba of course & Ikea
Down the stadium, there'll be no beer
Get down the Coopers or the Railway
Before the game with your mates, and have your say
Will he start with Ki Sung-Yueng
What's for certain, all our songs will be sung
Thursday nights... Channel 5?
A taxi home, don't drink and drive
The game is being shown on TV
But get yourself down to the Liberty
It's 730pm ITV 4
Everyone wants to be part of our European tour

Imagine if we get through to the Group Stage
The banter will be flying on the Cardiff/Swansea Facebook page
Are you as excited as me ?
Is Europe ready for the Jack Army
It's almost time Football is back
Stand up, sing up, and feel proud to be a JACK

Took a lot of stick for this one, its just banter

Your fans sang your going to win the league
You say we're obsessed but we are intrigued
How are you going to cope with the big boys
It's all gone quiet, no Cardiff City noise
2 up against Brentford
We laughed when Paul Hayes scored
For Cardiff yet another blow
Did they wear lucky Red or yellow
No wonder no one wants to sign
Can you imagine the cricket scores when it's Premier League time
Brentford 3 Cardiff City 2
We can't stop laughing at you
Red, and Yellow, pink and green, orange and purple too
A Cardiff City rainbow, Cardiff city rainbow, doesn't contain a trace of blue

Playing with Lee Trundle

You can imagine I was bursting with pride
To have Lee Trundle play for my side
To share a pitch, it's like a dream
And I'm like the cat, that's got the cream
More tricks than Dynamo,
A gentleman, An Ambassador
An Icon, the Entertainer
He can play when he wants, its a no brainer
He can wear black, even though we wear white
To me he is Mr Monday Night.
Unbelievable turns and flicks
Was the ball glued to his feet? the way that it sticks
I lost count of how many goals he scored
By all of Swansea he is adored
A left foot like a rocket
Too tricky to fit into any defenders pocket
He scores another worldie, even the opposition claps
To see him pull on those magic daps
Four defenders at once, and he dances through
Then he pulled the trigger and into the top corner it flew
He trapped the ball between his belly and thigh
I couldn't do that, no matter how many times I try
At times he was being marked by three or four men
To get it off him , they would have needed ten
Shoulder rolls, amazing control
I'd call him a master, with a football
The tricks I haven't got the words to explain
To have the talent and ability, to match the football brain
Unbelievable quick feet
With him in our team we ain't getting beat
He floats like a butterfly stings like a bee
Swansea's answer to Muhammad Ali
It's like something out of FIFA 13
After two games, and his hair was still pristine
To get to see him that close up
If I was Laudrup, I'd sign him up

He's back at home, the place he loves is Swansea
I'd love to see him tear the Premier League up, at the Liberty
He's a bundle of tricks
Will he score with a bicycle or overhead kicks
Next time I'm looking forward to the next trick bundle
An absolute pleasure and a privilege to play with Lee Trundle

www.Scfc.co.uk

There's a website called Scfc2.co.uk
Where you can sign up and have your say
All you have to be is a Swans fan
You can express your opinion
A great feature is Guestbook
Log on and take a look
Join in with Swans fans from around the world
Doesn't matter if you're a boy or a girl
There's guest blogs from fans like me
Where you can discuss all things Swansea City
We are Wales number one
Come join in the forum
It's really simple to register
Then your opinions you can share
Come on you shouldn't need much more persuasion
We wont discriminate if you're a Cardiff Malaysian
You know that Cardiff are poor
And jealous that we are on a European Tour
All you have to do to have your say
Is log onto www.scfc2.co.uk

Swansea 4 F.C Malmo 0

Twenty two years and we are back in Europe
A win and a clean sheet was my hope
Home debuts for the new boys
A worried spectator ? In David Moyes
Pitch side before the game, Gus Poyet & Brian Flynn
Then A slip let Michu in
A break through, we had got our rewards
The celebration, then the customary kick to the advertising boards
I enjoyed Bony's link up play
He leaps like he's from the NBA
To open his account, A headed goal
All our players look comfortable on the ball
Jonjo Shelveys passing range and his delivery
Looks a great signing for Swansea
Off the post from Michu and a tap in for Bony
His legs are the size of a 100 year oak tree
Ben Davies put on a great show
A brilliant team goal finished off by Pozuelo
I never thought we'd score four
Fair play to the away fans from FC Malmo
They sang and danced in the stand
They clapped and sang words I couldn't quite understand
I can't speak Swedish
A comfortable win, we got our wish
A 4-0 lead to take over there
Michu and Bony what a pair
The football we play, attractive for sure
Winning new fans, on our European Tour
Some of the lads showed signs of fatigue
A great start to our campaign of the Europa League
On his debut Wilfried Bony scored a double
Bony & Michu will cause a lot of defenders trouble

Not going to Sweden

All the Jacks on twitter wishing they had gone
To watch the Swans grace the surface of the Swedbank Stadion,
We'll play our way and show the Swedes
We belong in the pot of the Europa League seeds
I'm one of the thousands not in Malmo
So I'll watch the action unfold on Itv4
And see how many the Super Swans can score
Into the next round, we are sailing through
A strike force of Bony & Michu
There's only just over a thousand, but they'll sing loud,
The team make the Jack Army proud
@itvfootball will have a good night
I wish all the traveling Jacks, a safe return flight

Swans v Man U

Now Malmo are out of the way
We can all look forward to Saturday
Sky Sports SNF comes to town
Manchester United begin the defence of their crown
The sky cameras and Dave Jones we welcome to the Liberty,
Will the build up include Ash's incident with Robin Van Persie
Jamie Redknapp thinks we are top six, and could even make the top four
Will we hear his opinion on the start of our European Tour?
Premier League football is back
Sing up, and show you're proud to be a Jack
The Liberty will be bouncing
Hymns and Arias we will sing
We welcome the defending champions
The history of the Premier League shows they're the Top Guns
Lets create a cauldron of noise
Man United first league game managed by David Moyes
They've lost Sir Alex a managerial God
And we've certainly improved our squad
The players that have come in
Have the mentality to go for the win
If you can't get to the game to attend
Sit back, relax, it's Sky Sports free weekend
A game to launch Sky's new show, Saturday Night Football
Michel Vorm will start in goal
Our starting back four
Rangel, Ben Davies, Ash & Chico
Michael Laudrup has a selection headache
In midfield, he has some decisions to make
Leon Britton or Jose Canas ?
Both can tackle, both can pass
De Guzman, Ki or Jonjo Shelvey ?
Opinion's vary, it's Leon & Jonjo for me
Routledge on the left, to start ahead of Pablo
Dyer or Pozuelo ?
Dyers has got the pace
Pozuelo drifts inside, he will create space.
Michu and Bony up top
Rio and Vidic will be trying to stop

I'm excited as Man United and the Swans cross swords
Will Michu score and kick the advertising boards
I don't know who will start
He could go with Monk or Amat
Neil Taylor only now getting a mention
All of our players are in contention
You will all have a different opinion to me
But we are all part of the Jack Army
Michael Laudrup is cooler than the Fonz
Man U, "Your only here to watch the Swans "
Man United at home, we are in Europe, pinch me is this a dream ?
Watching Michael Laudrup assemble his Fantasy Football DreamTeam.

Transfer Deadline Day

Will Arsenal and United get their way
Big clubs wanting time to stand still
Is there time for Fellani and Ozil ?
Big money deals will they go through
Players dreams could still come true
I could watch the drama all night
The excitement unfolds as we watch Jim White
Will your club come in for a late steal
Is there time to do a deal
Players, fans try to guess
Not us cos we've signed Vasquez

Cardiff sign Odenwingie

After spending all night in his car
Then realised he wasn't even wanted by QPR
Congratulations Cardiff , you signed Peter Odenwingie
He could rescue the fans in his rubber dingy
They can hang on to him as they swim away
The only club dull enough to match demands for his pay
He's a West Bromwich Albion outcast
Cardiff fans love talking about their past
They still talk about 1927 when they won the FA cup
On derby day, we'll finally get to shut them up
A footballing lesson, waiting to be taught
"You're just a small town in Newport"
An away win at Legoland
Swansea City " Take my hand,
Take my whole life too"
"You used to wear blue
Now you wear Red
You look like twats, when you slap your head"
Can you imagine how rich I will be,
When I sell Cardiff Arm Bands outside the Liberty
Go with the tide, down stream in the River Tawe
You'll know where you are when you reach the Swansea Bay sea
In February when we send you back down
Vincent Tan sells up, and moves onto a new town
A new owner comes in, and your future looks bright
He'll build you up in Black & White

Jonjo's night

Liverpool arrived at the Liberty
Monday Night Football on Sky TV
A dream start as a Shelvey left footer and the ball hits the net
I had him to score first, on Sky Bet
We were still singing his name
Then a back pass, and he held his head in shame
One minute he's our hero
Then in a flash, he's down to zero
A lot of the fans were having a moan
The East Stand made sure, he'd "Never walk alone"
They carried on singing to show him support
Still thinking about his dream start, then he got caught
He played in Sturridge to equalise
To be in the dressing room half time and be one of the flies
What is Laudrup going to say
We sat too deep, and allowed them to play

Ashley Williams in a challenge with Steven Gerrard
He's big and he's fuckin hard
Shoulder to shoulder and Ash didn't flinch
Two national captains, wouldn't give away an inch
Both trying to knock the wind from out of the others sails
He's "Ashley Williams, He's Captain of Wales"
Another stray pass from Shelvey gave Moses the ball
He ran from the half way line to score Liverpool's second goal
I think the first half performance we let them have it, and we sat too deep
Sloppy in possession, the ball we need to keep
Start of the second half, I was surprised to see Jonjo
I hope we come out, and have a real go…
Then with 63 minutes gone,
Ash, to Chico, Chico to Leon
Leon to Rangel with a little one-two
Passing and probing looking for a way through
De Guzman to Shelvey,
Then Shelvey onto Bony
Bony to Leon across the grass with a zip
Leon with a forward chip

Shelvey with a head down to Michu's feet
The Capacity crowd out of our seat

"He scores when he wants, He scores when he wants,
Miguel Michu, he scores when he wants"
An eleven pass move finished with a goal
Proud Jacks standing tall
"They don't sing your name, they don't sing your name
Brendan Rogers, they don't sing your name "

Jonjo had the character to come back & after the game apologise,
Man of the Match in many people's eyes
Ashley Williams man of the match for me
A night to remember for Jonjo Shelvey
The programme cover had it right
The story book was about Jonjo's night
A game of football highs and lows
Coming back from those bitter blows
Spirit, Character and just 21
A story to tell to his unborn daughter or son
The night Jonjo Shelvey was trending on twitter worldwide

A comeback which left us bursting with pride
Determination, team spirit and lots of fight
A good game, and a roller coaster night
If Liverpool fans had been happy they'd have sung You'll
Never Walk Alone and held aloft their scarves
A cliche but it was a game of two halves
Swansea v Liverpool a very special game for me
One that he'll never forget, Jonjo Shelvey
In the goals he had a part in all four
As Swansea & Liverpool battled out a two all draw
The first team to score and take points of Liverpool FC
I'm proud of the players, like the whole of Swansea

Leon

We were just getting over the Tony Petty disease
The club were struggling
We were down on our knees
We'd just got rid of the Australian clown
But we were on the verge of going down
Then Leon Britton, signed on loan
To me at the time, he was virtually unknown
Last game of the season we played Hull City
We needed leaders, not self pity
That game we won 4-2
And we began to fall in love with you
If you were there like me, you'll remember the game
Over ten years and we chant his name
Leon, Leon, Leon
Someone we can rely on
He wins the ball and breaks up play
He can pass the ball all day
In the Divisions he's played for us in all four
And he's part of our European tour

He's only 5 foot 6
If I were Roy Hodgson he'd be one of my picks
Maybe he should come and watch from the West Stand
Cos I Can't believe he's never played for England

Cardiff Premier League start

You opened up away to West Ham
It wasn't long and your toys were thrown out of the pram
You didn't manage a single shot on goal
A turn and finish from Joe Cole
Behind the ball, you always had ten
I loved seeing Kevin Nolan's celebratory chicken
You celebrated a loss, cos you were higher than us
We'd play Man United, but aren't ones to fuss
Then you had Man City I'll be honest I expected a cricket score
I thought 7 nil, where Aguero hits four
So I've got to give credit where credit is due
How you beat Man City, I haven't a clue ?
I wondered against the big boys, how you'd cope
An historic win to give you hope
A double from Frazier Campbell
Where you will finish, it's too early to tell.
Both clubs have improved in different ways
You are all now praying that, Vincent Tan stays
To quote a song, He took something perfect, and painted it red
Your all loosing brain cells, every time you tap your head
What some of you boys in Cardiff, would do for five dollar?
Bend over for Vincent, and do the Ayatollah
They talked about Cardiff's incredible noise
They've moved on from Davie Jones and two little boys
Seriously though, All jokes aside
After a 3-2 win, you are bursting with pride
Sky Sports camera men all rang in sick the next day
All with stiff necks, they can't wait til next May.
Where you will go down
Get you're snorkel and flippers on, so you don't drown
We know you love to swim away
It happens on every derby day
The way Cardiff fans are going on, Champions they'll be crowned
If only they could keep the ball on the ground
I think it's great that after one win, they've got some hope
We all know what was said when Cardiff City went to Rome to see the Pope
They'd beaten Man City, instead of celebrating , they cared what I might think ?
It's not my fault, the Bluebird is extinct
You should have celebrated a win in your lucky red kit
But they wanted to tweet the Jack Poet
Write us a poem about us beating Man City and you haven't got a point
So this is for you, I'm not one to disappoint
I wrote a few Cardiff poems, a month ago
You'd beaten Man City, and now you want more!

They were number one on google, as no one knew their name
They'd forgotten, they marched in protest, before that very game
Now all of a sudden they love Vincent Tan
Everyone loves red, and everyone's a fan

Cardiff fans say I'm obsessed, but I'm just making fun
It's route one football, they remind me of Wimbledon.
Cardiff fans are like The Wombles they love rubbish too
But Wellington the Womble, is original, he still wears his famous blue
Now you can welcome Everton
Roberto Martinez, that should be fun
To Wales I hope you welcome him back
Remember Roberto is a Jack
Some of you may not care,
Tell me what colour Everton wear ?
You all know, you should be wearing blue,
It's ironic that your firm was called the Soul Crew
Did they disappear as Cardiff sold their Soul,
Did Tan offer them redundancy or are they just on the dole ?
Carry on, keep running your mouth
We are kings of Welsh football, you're like Queen of the South
Can you imagine at the derby if all Swans fans wore blue
At least they'd work out who is waiting for you
It's 9 weeks and we begin to countdown
Don't forget your arm bands, we don't want you to drown
We will show you a football masterclass
The football is designed to be played on the grass
That day there will be a reality check
I'm taking a cushion to support my neck
That day for Welsh football the atmosphere will be brill
We'll go 3 up, and sing is this a fire drill
And from that day you'll always Remember,
Remember Remember The Third of November.

Swans Dreaming

It started way back in 1912
Look at what we've achieved, and pinch yourself
Now we are all living the dream
That's not the way it's always been
In a packed Liberty We sing " Take my hand"
Think back to the original Centre (South) Stand.
Back in the day it was formed on a mound
Where some concrete & railway sleepers could be found
That place I first stood when I was four years old
Soaking wet and freezing cold
To that I have my big sister to thank
For taking me to stand on the North Bank
That was back in 1981
Toshack & Curtis in Division One
We had many famous names
Take a minute and remember Robbie James
He was my hero back in the day
In the days before The Swansea Way
He had a shop at the bottom of Clase
I'd play football round the back of the Mace
Remember the big clock, please try ?
Standing on the North Bank, til the day I die
We thought we were black and white dynamite
Across the stand in bold white
Welcome to Swansea City A.F.C
We were way down by the sea
As you walked towards the turnstile, barbed wire running above
I couldn't stop myself, falling in love....

You would have had one of the meat pies
Swansea City, The Fall and Rise
It hurt every time, we got beat
Lee Trundle, he has Magic feet
Unbelievable close control
Who could forget that shoulder roll
A showboat, what a trick
James Thomas hatrick
 The yellow ball, touch line shoveled to clear snow
The last goal scored there by Robbo
Look around, there's a lot of rust
In the day we didn't have Huw to trust

In May 2005 we had to say goodbye
We are Swansea, Swansea til I die
Standing on the North Bank with our arms above our head and outstretch
We are all going to miss The Vetch
From the Vetch Field to the Liberty
We will follow Swansea City

In the Cardiff slums

If you're a Cardiff City fan it's really not that funny
You can't attract players even though you try to pay big money
You may have your Malaysian coin
It's a pity no one wants to join
Malaysian currency is called Ringgit
The problem being everyone knows, you're shit
Cardiff's a shambles, but where to begin
No matter who you bid for, you cant bring anyone in
Apart from a Danish striker Andreas Cornelius
His boyhood hero, is managed by us
If he was any good Laudrup would know
Tom Ince isn't the only one, to tell you boys no
Your first Premier League game is away to West Ham,
Cardiff City , is an absolute sham
West Ham will be forever blowing bubbles
Your fans will bring shame, always causing troubles
Your owner has made you a laughing stock
We all know Craig Bellamy is an absolute cock
He brought a book out, but not many Cardiff fans can read
Up in Cardiff where you all interbreed
Your father is your brother
And your sister is your mother
Thats a typical Cardiff family.
When you visit the Liberty
You kick the ball long, we will shout.... ooof
Sales of armbands will have gone through the roof
Its embarrassing the way you play
And your fans that swim away
You sing "We're coming for you"
Cardiff City will you wear blue ?
The call from the swimming pool tannoy,
"All swimmers wearing redbird bands"
It's a long way to run to the Swansea Bay sands
Put your armbands on, we don't want you to drown
"Cardiff City's falling down"

You used to be called the Bluebirds
Your about as hard as one of my turds
I wonder how they'll cope with the big occasion
I know you're all proud, to call yourself Malaysian
You're getting relegated that's for sure
Whilst we are off on a European Tour
Mark Hudson running his mouth, to deflect that he's gay
We are still waiting for him to be charged by the FA
He's been inside his fair share of bums
So many willing receivers to choose from, in the Cardiff slums
The top cuisine in the slums is a dead rat
Now, Tap your head , if you're a twat

Valencia V Swans

It dominated my Facebook and my Twitter feed
I'm not off to Valencia, am I jealous ? Indeed
We could have more Spaniards than them on the field
We will have to wait until the teams are revealed
The atmosphere will be electric in the Mestalla
Jacks drinking San Miguel instead of a Stella
Sangria & Sun
Enjoying life following Wales number one
Returning to Valencia an ex player in Pablo,
Is he fit? , to run the show
We could be more Spanish than Valencia
Señoritas and plenty of beer
We've got our own Spanish Matador
We all love Chico our number four
The squad could stay at Pablos old house, we won't need a hotel
At the back Chico , Amat and Rangel
In the middle the boy can tackle and he can pass
There's only one Jose Canas
I'm sure our Spanish Armada will be eager
To showcase against a team from La Liga
Will Pozuelo start on the right
Proud to play in Swansea's Black & White
A debut for Alvaro Vasquez ?
Coming off the bench is my guess
I would be happy with a draw
And elated if we can score
Who are we ? Jack Army that's who
I'm backing our number 9, Miguel Michu
A safe journey to every single traveling Jack
I hope you bring all three points back
8 Spaniards in our squad, each one an ace,
Then onto Selhurst Park, for three points against Palace
I'm addicted to Swansea City, and there's no cure
I'm jealous I'm not there on our European Tour

Swansea win and Cardiff loose

On Thursday we beat Valencia 3 nil away
Then a few days later on the Sunday
We traveled to play Crystal Palace
A debut for Varquez, our young Spanish ace
Michu got us underway
A dream start, no more to say
The Swans have been on fire
A finish from Nathan Dyer
2-0 another away win
Just as your lot, were peering out of the bin
The last six days we've played 3 games
You welcomed Spurs, with their big names
Themselves they played in Europe too
Another team to play in Cardiff wearing blue
It is a blue, although it's dark
They played and passed you off the park
Early on you had a great chance
Lloris handled outside the box, at a glance
Frazier Campbell through one on one
No shots on target, can't be fun
Cardiff fans will say I've got an obsession
At home you get very little possession
If you're happy with that, then that's your call
8,9,10,11 men behind the ball
Your keeper fair play was as busy as a bee
Then Pauliniho in minute ninety three
I've never felt more like singing the blues
When Swansea win and Cardiff loose

West Ham 3 Cardiff 2

An away trip to Upton Park
The rats are scurrying in the dark
Cardiff City are a sham
Getting beaten again by West Ham
20 seconds and they began to un "Ravel"
Vincent Tan is Malaysian's answer to Jimmy Saville
Matt Jarvis puts them two up
Cardiff City are heading out of the cup
Out before Swansea have begun a title defence
One word sums it up.....immense
2 nil down, time to move the bus
They cant even rely on Andreas Cornelius
All that money that has been spent
How many more boys, could Tan have rent?
Supporting Cardiff can't be much fun
They get one back thanks to No-one

Odenwinge scores to equalise
Cardiff City, a comeback surprise?
On Facebook & Twitter, they all piped up
You'd swear they'd won the FA cup
1927, was a long time ago
They like to talk about what happened before
They call themselves the best team in Wales
You know the Swansea blueprint and what it entails
Odenwinge came for the big pay
Then up popped Richard Vaz Te
Even more late heart break
How much more can you scummers take?
I was impressed that you'd fought back
Will Malkay be next for the sack?
The league table shows you're on a downward slide
Swansea City play with pride
You are out, of the League Cup
And at us, you're forever looking up
The Bluebirds, no more, it's just a myth
So Lets all laugh at Cardiff

Birmingham 3 Swansea 1

So the defending champions were beaten by Birmingham ,
A disappointing performance, 3 goals to one
They'd been away to Valencia in Spain
Onto London, then Birmingham in the rain
Our boys haven't had a chance for a rest
It's fair to say, they weren't at their best
When you play against champions, Everyone ups their game
Out in the fourth round, a bit of a shame
It could be a blessing in disguise
But Birmingham beating Swansea, came as a surprise
We went out to a championship team
4 games in ten days, and the boys ran out of steam
We aren't complaining we are the victims of our own success,
We aren't like Cardiff City, and in a right mess
What would happen to you're club if Tan walked away?
Put that on your forum, I wonder what you'd say
Before you run your mouth, have a little think
Your next owner, may make you play in pink
"We build it up in Black & White"
Tradition, Values and we do everything right
A blueprint on how a club should be run
Simply known as Wales Number One.
Ten years ago, we were bought for just a pound,
Are Cardiff City in the draw for the fifth round ?
Cardiff loosing to West Ham is the norm
Any poem mentioning Cardiff goes down a storm.
There are decent people in Cardiff, but they've got more than their fair share of scum
The Jack Poet is a topic On Cardiff City's forum,
Just for you to know, I'm writing poems for a book
It's so easy winding you lot up, you jump straight on the hook
One minute they tell me, not to write anymore, and I'm obsessed
Then the Swans loose, and I'm getting poem requests
A poem is sometimes called a ditty
I've done one for you, when you beat Manchester City
It will be in the book
A famous day for Cardiff, when the premier league shook
I support the Swans, in Wales we are number one,
Learn to take some banter, it's just a bit of fun

The last one in the book will be about the Welsh derby
It'll be out for Christmas , so buy it for your
family....
Your sister is your mother
Your father is your brother
In Wales, Cardiff you are the best
At a game you all love, its called incest.

Swansea v Arsenal

Saturday night live on Talksport
A game for the purist, one would have thought
We welcome Talksport to broadcast live from the Liberty
Arsenal take on Swansea City
I'm looking forward to Saturday
Two teams who want to play the right way
The passing is sure to be sublime
You can listen to the commentary on Medium Wave 1089
Swans v Arsenal it will be like watching Brazil
We will have to keep a close eye on Mesut Özil
Will Özil get another assist
It's certainly a game, not to be missed
Or will he slip into Leon Britton's back pocket
A good game, every time the two sides have met
Michu to score the first goal
Upset the Gunners, who are on a roll
Will Jack Wilshere be tired, now he's a dad, he's been up all night,
Will Laudrup get the tactics right
I think it could end up finishing three, three
I hope we don't end up discussing the referee
Share your opinion or just listen in
Bony to score last and Swans get the win
Will Wenger make Adrian Durham's "heads gone"
Talksport is second to none
What other predictions are there for the score?
After the game on your way home, Call Collymore
Monday morning drive to work listening to Alan Brazil
But will we be talking about Michu or Özil

Credit to Cardiff

Fair play to Cardiff they've impressed me
They lost to West Ham, but bounced back to beat Man City
I couldn't believe they won that game 3-2
A great result, fair play to you
A Draw at home to Everton
Another point away to Hull, One :One
It's all about getting points on the board
That goal by Mutch against Fulham, the best goal you've scored ?
I'll be honest I didn't think you'd cope
But the start that they've had will give them all hope
Unlucky against Spurs, with a late break of heart
I take my hat off to you, its a really good start

To win away from home at Craven Cottage
Holding their own, on the Premier League stage
This game is all about getting results
To write a Cardiff poem without slipping in any insults
It was quite hard to do
You've won my respect, so well done to you

Supporters behave

The Welsh derby is on the third of November
I hope it's a game that we will all remember
Will Sky be back for more?
It's just a short trip, up the M4
Lets hope the derby is trouble free
People want to go along and enjoy as a family
Fierce rivals on the pitch
Lets hope it happens without a hitch
The hooligans need to stay away
The real fans want to have a good day
It's just a short trip up the road
If the fans behave, its us, the players will applaud

A first ever Premier League Welsh derby
On sky sports for the world to see
We want them talking about the beautiful game
Not a minority of fans, trying to bring shame
The atmosphere will be bouncing
With their hearts both fans will try to out sing
Neither teams will want to give an inch away
Swansea will want to get it down and play
Playing With passion, Committed tackles
The groan of the crowd when the crossbar rattles
Local bragging rights at stake
Stay away, if it's trouble you plan to make
There could be red cards, and many a booking
But behave yourselves as the world will be watching
Who will come out on top as Wales number one
A message to both sets of supporters, stay away scum
Plenty of banter before, during and after
Show yourself to be a true football supporter
So support and get behind your side
A Welsh derby to fill you with pride
Famous for Choirs and Rugby
Daffodils, Dragons and the Mining Industry
Does anyone really know why we hate each other so much?
I'm not expecting us to make up and all have a cwtch

Lava Bread, Cockles and Cawl
A yellow card could come out, at the very first foul
Whether you support Cardiff and Malky MacKay
Or part of Michael Laudrup's Army, and your Swansea til you die
If you're looking for trouble don't come along
If you want to get at the opposition, do it with a song
Whether its were coming / waiting for you
Or you used to be blue.

Lets hope there's no arrests and little fuss
One things for certain, Cardiff will park the bus
You're the Capital City, and rightly so
We are showcasing Europe, on a European Tour
Look at what lessons our children are being taught
That Cardiff is just a small town in Newport
I don't think Swansea & Cardiff will ever class the other as a friend
Thankfully in the middle is Neath, Port Talbot & Bridgend
I'm not expecting us to suddenly unite
But act like grown ups, and don't come for a fight
So if you are going to the Cardiff City stadium
We will find out who is Wales number one
Enjoy the game and the big occasion
But don't damage your clubs reputation

Match day Vorm

Off for a pint, cos It's match day
What team will Laudrup start with today
The players walk out, and we sing loud
Follow the Swans, they make us proud
Hymns and Arias sung with pride
Stand up, sing loud, arms aloft and opened wide
Hairs stand up on the back of my neck
"Your only here to watch the Swans" as we give the away team a little peck
The noise erupts as the players huddle
Pumped up from the pep talk and cuddle
The Swans are playing well, and on top form
Hollands number one, Michele Vorm

Michu

After taking the Premier League by storm
A call up reward for his run of form
He is set to link up with World Champions, Spain
In the Europa League he bled, and played through the pain
It's unbelievable, £2 million is all that he cost
And now he had the nod from Del Bosque
In ahead of Llorente and Soldado
The experience will help him to grow
Iniesta, Xavi, Fabregas
Rubbing shoulders with players that are World Class
I'm sure you'll settle in just fine
Representing Spain, Swansea City's number nine
He's Swansea City's player of the year
Lift your hand bend your fingers and wave to your ear
I hope you get on and you score a goal
Felicitaciones mi amigo Español
Good Luck from everyone at Swansea City
I hope you score one, but I think you'll get three
Michu's still improving under Michael Laudrup
He's dreaming he can play in the World Cup
If you support Swansea City you'll also support Spain
They've got Sun & Sangria, and we take the rain
This poem is all about you
Miquel Miquel Michu
He's got Belarus and Georgia on his mind
Miguel Pèrez Cuesta you are one of a kind

The Painters in

This story cannot be true
A painter and decorator, Cardiff's new number two
He came to help paint Cardiff red
He ended up becoming an inbred
I laughed so hard, tears I cry
A new right hand man, for Malkay MacKay
He's now Scouting for Vincent Tan
Thank God I'm not a Cardiff fan
Can Cardiff fans take any more of this shit
Has this guy, even got a work permit ?
Has this made Malkays position untenable
Is Vincent Tan, mentally stable ?
He's treating Cardiff City like its a toy
Now he's introduced us to his new Rent Boy
Malkays left scratching instead of tapping his head
His number two won't bring a ball to training, but a brush and roller set instead
They say he's Tan's Son's friend
When will this farce, ever end
Do we have to wait until he goes broke
He's turned Cardiff City into an absolute joke
You all slap your heads, if I'm honest it makes you look like a bit of a twat
Your new manager will end up being Borat

Ashley Williams

He leads us out every game
He's our Captain, we sing his name
The ref flips the coin, calls heads or tails
He's Ashley Williams, he's Captain of Wales

Able to anticipate the strikers runs
And not afraid to mix it with the big guns
Gerrard, Andy Carroll or RvP
He's the captain of Swansea City
He leads by example and doesn't give an inch
A player squares up, and he doesn't flinch
Van Persie's head he almost took
Sir Alex is that in your book ?
Off Cardiff fans he takes some stick
Swansea City's number six
Before kick off he gets the team in a huddle,
Together, committed roused from his team cuddle
Our Captain and a Leader in every way
And for a Centre Half, the boy can play
He's the rock at the back
Proud to be a Jack

Building up to the Derby

I'm sure everyone is as nervous as me
The biggest Welsh Derby in history
The excitement has been building all week
Swans travel to Cardiff, and it's three points we seek
All the real fans, hoping it happens, with no trouble
Avoiding all bridges in a trip called a bubble
A Local Derby watched worldwide
Two teams battling for Welsh pride
Cardiff City's falling down
Vincent Tan what an absolute clown
Of that most Cardiff fans will agree
And I'm not very popular in the Capital City
Malky is spineless he's lacking backbone
He'll be replaced by an Electrician from Sierra Leone
How on earth can he take so much shit?
The painter didn't even have a work permit

No real manager would tolerate being undermined
The word Yellow springs to mind
& Red like your faces embarrassed how your club is run
So easy for us Jacks, to make fun
This isn't about the three points, but the bragging right
Cardiff's falling down, We'll build it up in Black and White

Derby Day

It's going to be a cauldron of noise
One to separate the men from the boys
I thought I'd slip in one more peck
Kick off time the hairs will stand up on the back of my neck
When Mike Dean blows the whistle and gets the game started
It's not going to be one, for the faint hearted
The atmosphere will be electric
Which team will Laudrup pick?
Everyone will have an opinion on what they think
It will be 100mph so try not to blink
Tackles will be flying in
Both sets of fans demanding a win
This game is too close to call
Will Cardiff see much of the ball
Two cities separated by 48 miles
Two sides with contrasting styles
One build on the foundation of the supporters trust
Ten years ago, we almost went bust
The other run by a billionaire
Their fans don't mind what colour they wear
One team that like to get it on the floor and play
The other who hoof it in the air, and then pray
A formation with one in attack
And that just leaves, the ten at the back
Mark Hudson was running his mouth acting hard
On the bench again, you scum bastard
Your contract they aren't going to renew
We're laughing at you, we're laughing at you, Mark Hudson, we're laughing at you
Both sets of fans will be going berserk
Wanting the bragging rights, for Monday in work
If Cardiff win, I'll expect a backlash
On Twitter the scum will be talking trash
I've got a feeling Cardiff will go quiet
When we are 3 up, I predict a riot

It's all set for an explosive Derby Day
Michu scores the winner and celebrates with a Swim Away
Bring on the banter, and the abuse cos I enjoy it
Lots of Love, The Jack Poet

More Derby Build Up

The tension is beginning to mount
Each player will want to make every tackle count
A Welsh derby watched worldwide
To find out in Wales, who are the best side
Separated by 38 miles of the M4
I'm backing Michu to score
Derbies like Glasgow, Milan, Merseyside
Battling it out, for local pride
Thank God we don't have to share our City
Look at their women, they aren't very pretty
Suffering for their inbred sins
And in out of dustbins
Looking for something to eat
Six Fingers, and Web feet
Michael Laudrup has mentioned it like an El Classico
Tempers in this one, are likely to soar
Big tackles going in hard
Will we see a straight red card
Can you get the ball off us ?
Can we get in behind that bus
For Wales it's a huge occasion
We'll fly the Welsh flag, you fly the Malaysian
The Ayatollah you took from Iran
Lebanese Chairman Sam Hamman
You sold your soul, you'd sell your Nan
How sad it must be, to be a Cardiff fan
You can scream an obscenity
Vincent Tan has taken your identity
We know who we are, we know who we are
The Pride of Wales, the best team by far
Will you get to 40% possession ?
2-0 to the Swans, sends Cardiff deeper into depression
All you lot go on about is attendance
You haven't realised Tan has pulled down your pants
He's bent you over, and given you a dry one

We stood up to Tony Petty, and made him run
Before and after games, you should march and shout
All you can do is hash tag Tan Out
Banter and trading many an insult
Sunday is all about the result
The winner will have local bragging rights
We won't change our colours, our famous black and Whites
You've even had the painters in
Tan took your insides, and just left you shelled in your skin
What's next for Cardiff floated on the Malaysian stock exchange ?
What else can Vincent Tan change
Please don't throw your spare change at Mike Dean
Red, and Yellow, Pink & Green
Orange and Purple too
A Cardiff City Rainbow, Cardiff City rainbow, doesn't contain a trace of blue

We are all on a countdown to this Sunday
Bony to score the winner, and do the Swim Away
Something you need to know about Vincent Tan
He's taking the piss, he's a Swansea City Fan
A famous win for Swansea City
Will send you into the bottom three
After the game, will he sack Malkay McKay?
Vincent Tan is Swansea, Swansea til I die

So now you want a Poem

So the fans of Cardiff are now asking for a poem
You can't pick and choose when I write them
Maybe I could become Cardiff's Official Poet Laurette
Work for a club millions in debt
There's no doubt you deserved the win
But can you please stay out of my bin
You managed to scrape a one nil
There wasn't a lot of skill
Lets be honest it was a poor game
Not one to go in the Welsh derby hall of fame
Medel was meant to be a pitbull ?
Softer than a ball of wool
He went down easier than my Mrs, after a bottle of wine
If he was my player, I'd issue him a two week wage fine
I wouldn't show I was hurt, but that's just me
Get up and get on with it, you fucking pansie
Swans fans can have no complaints
Of all the players to score
Outmuscling our number four
Steven Caulker big respect to you for not celebrating
He wants to be an extra in a "Jack to a King"
With 5 minutes left, and then he sent off Vorm
Against a decent side, a new asshole would have been torn
Ten men and our full back in goal
Cardiff have no clue how to move the ball
It's time to move on and not dwell
A message to Cardiff, You'll never beat the Rangel

The Fall out/ Stick together

We are all down after the defeat in the Welsh Derby
It's not that bad supporting Swansea City
Look how far we've come
After Sunday we are all feeling numb
Attacking our own players & manager verbally
That's not the way forward, not for me
That's not what social media is for
Not designed for an internal Twitter war
They are our players, we would normally applaud
Lets not turn on each other, and implode
We lacked passion, heart and fight
But I'm backing Laudrup & Co to put things right
Reading things on Twitter , I need a bit of a cull
Think back to when we had to beat Hull
We stuck by them we believed
At the moment we are feeling bereaved
Fans need to get behind the boys
Make the Liberty a cauldron of noise
Europa League we beat Valencia away
November the 3rd not a great day
Put on Swansea City the fall and rise
Shut your mouth and open your eyes
Supporting Swansea City isn't all bad
Think of the great times we've had
A couple of games and we will bounce back
Be proud that you were born a Jack
At Swansea we all need to stick together and unite
Continue our journey in the top flight
Like me you're hurt and feeling down
We aren't being run by Tan the clown
Cardiff fans were happy with how their team played
All they did was put up a blockade
Their game plan is based on trying not to concede
We all know that tactic isn't going to succeed
Hoping to score from a corner or free kick
Compare them to Wimbledon or Stoke, take your pick
They've no identity , they have no colour
Could their play be any duller

It's time to move on and draw a line in the sand
Swansea City take my hand

I'm gutted, I'm not going to lie
But I am Swansea, Swansea til I die
Ups and downs the rough with the smooth
We can't change a thing, so on we move
Lets send the players to Russia with love
Back your team, when push comes to shove
Get behind, and support your team
We are living out a Swansea City dream
Our Players need a lift from the crowd
And I know the players will do us proud

Ramsay scores, and you applaud

Would they sing Aron Ramsays name ?
Or boo him like Ryan Giggs and bring more shame
A Cardiff boy booed by the Canton End
The mans a living Welsh legend,
So a homecoming for a Cardiff City scholar
In the game singing "Ramsay do the Ayatollah"
How could Ramsay pay them back ?
Bang one in , in the next attack
Classy, that he didn't celebrate
A player that's gone from good to great
PFA player of the year ? he can't stop scoring,
If I have to watch Cardiff I can't stop snoring
They build a wall, they park the bus
They cannot pass the ball like us,
Defend at all cost, try and nick a goal
A style of play? They sold their soul
Cheering an opposition goal, something's wrong ?
Adrian Durham said it best " heads gone "
It's not right to you and me
No applause for Flamini
He did the Ayatollah, you got what you wanted
Confused with the colours yellow and red
Applauding an opposition goal, and even a standing ovation
You're all proud to be Malaysian
A Cardiff boy, a Welsh ace
Repaid Cardiff with a lovely brace
"He's one of your own, he's one of your own
Aaron Ramsay he's one of your own"
Today he made us Jacks all smile ....
A typical Cardiff family on Jeremy Kyle
DNA test, 'is my sister my mother ? '
Followed by 'is my father really my brother?'
Lie detector results revealed
Do you nod off, when Cardiff City take to the field
Boring Boring Cardiff, it's a snorefest
Stick to the game you love, and that's incest

10 years and its Hull again

Ten years ago we had to beat Hull
Supporting Swansea City is never dull
How times have changed since then
Thank God for the Swans Trust, Amen
We've gone from the Vetch Field to the Liberty
A roller coaster journey, with Swansea City
We've gone full circle and so have they
I hope they survive come what May
They are part of our history I suppose
Now managed by Steve Bruce and that nose
So come on Swans lets have an another 4-2
Then a win in St Gallen and we are sailing through

Crystal Palace two Cardiff nil

Crystal Palace two, Cardiff City nil
Leaving their seats, Is it a fire drill?
Strange that Cardiff fans didn't applaud
When one of their old boys scored
Well done Cameron Jerome
Can you do the same, when Cardiff are home
57% possession 2 shots on target
One that Cardiff fans will want to forget
You know you must be absolute crap
When you concede a goal scored by Marouane Chamakh
For Tony Pulis, a first home win
A relegation battle, your getting sucked in
Cardiff City, one win in the last nine
Hovering just above the relegation line
Your only win, came against Swansea
Now all you've got is our pity
Every other week humiliation
An embarrassment to the Welsh nation
Cardiff players hang your head in shame
They lost a 6 point game
Cos Cardiff City, love getting beat
An old boy with a clean sheet
Surely Gabbidon would " do the Ayatollah, Danny "
One word for Gary Medel.... Fanny
Ian Moody helping Palace up in the stand
He lost his job, down to the Re-brand

Ten years on

In Huw we know we are in safe hands
No colour changes or rebrands
For a £1 our club was bought
There's only one team in Wales, to support
Look at how far we've come,
Standing on the North Bank in sleet, hail, rain and sometimes some sun
Ten years ago we had little hope
From the game v Hull, to a film directed by Mal Pope
Who knows what else the future will bring
A blockbuster movie to look forward to ....A Jack to a King
Remember we have the quality and the class
And to all Jacks I wish you and your family a Merry Christmas

Pink Ferrari Crossbar Challenge

The players have a challenge to hit the crossbar
The looser has to drive a pretty shit car
Its called a Pink Ferrari
Who will take it for the M.O.T
Ben Davies driving around in week one
With all his team mates, making fun
Week 2 saw a head to head final between Pablo & Vorm
Taxed & insured, so no need for a Sorn
The vehicle is just about, fit for the road
The public will see a Swans player driving, and think is that all he can afford?
Vorm's effort clips the bar
Leaving Pablo Hernandez stuck with the car
He takes the players out for a spin
To drive that car, a Premier League player, must have pretty thick skin
Off cruising down the Kingsway
Then parked next to their house, in the driveway
Will he enjoy his week in the pink jeep
If you see it around, give it a beep
Will he jazz it up, and pimp his ride
Pulling up in training, he's lost his pride
This one is set to run and run
Good to see the players, having some fun
Players will work on pin point accuracy
Or forfeit and drive around in the Pink Ferrari

Swansea Dream Team
#DreamTeamJack

Who would make your Dream Team
If you had to pick from Swansea's cream
If you were in the pub, with some of your mates
Would you dream of a team of Alan Tates
Pick from history , past or present have your say
Freestone , Vorm or Willy Guret
Remember Dai Davies, Dai the cross
Who would you pick if you were the boss
You have to choose, don't go sitting on the fence
Angel Rangel or Wyndam Evans at Full back on the right of defence
At left back at number 3
Chris Coleman, Ben Davies bit too soon for me
Colin Irwin or Mark Clode
By the North Bank they are adored
We sing Hymns n Arias originally sung by Max Boyce
At centre half we are spoilt for choice
At 4 & 5 Who do you rate
Garry Monk, Ashley Williams or even Alan Tate
Or would you pair John Charles and Mel Nurse
In midfield Ferre Bodde if it wasn't for an injury curse
Leon Britton is the heart and soul for me
Would you play him next to Jan Molby ?
Or do we go back in time and use the Internet and search
And go for a legend in Ivor Allchurch
So many famous names...
Robbie and or Leighton James
Would you go with someone like Lampard or another of the loans
An FA Cup & League double winner in Cliff Jones
A Spanish International in Miquel Michu
Who would you choose it's up to you
A different opinion to mine ?
A ten in the hole ? Playing off nine
Or would you go with two up top in attack
Would you start with John Toshack

Would you play him with Alan Curtis, perhaps
Or Lee Trundle with his magic daps
Think about all the wonder goals he scored
Would he play well with Bob Latchford
You will all have an opinion different to me
Who would you pick for Dream Team Swansea
Come on Twitter and have a crack
Use the Hashtag #DreamTeamJack